Human Interest

Human Interest

Poems by

Kim Bridgford

Kelsay Books

Cover art: Pete Duval

ISBN 13: 978-0692629864

Kelsay Books
Aldrich Press
www.kelsaybooks.com

For Russell Goings, with profound thanks
for stopping by my office in 1995

Acknowledgments

Able Muse: "The Fence"

American Arts Quarterly: "Posting on the Wall, Facebook"

Angle: "Well, Pinch My Toes and Call Me a Jelly Doughnut"

First Things: "Juliet on Facebook"

The Hopkins Review: "Ghosting"

Kin: "Falling through the Cracks"

Light: "Oh, Rats"

Life and Legends: "Done," "Lindbergh Baby Kidnapping," "Patty Hearst Sonnet"

Measure: "Jumping," "Spite" (Reprint)

Poem: "Dictionary"

The Raintown Review: "Spite," "Telling It"

The Road Not Taken: "Perfection Is the Enemy of the Good"

The Rotary Dial: "Bad Writing," "Benign Neglect," "Gone Are the Libraries," "Misery Loves Company," "Nibbled to Death by Ducks," "No," "The Past," "Speaking Truth to Power"

South Carolina Review: "Unfriend"

Southwest Review: "Ventriloquist"

Theodate: "The Cyberspace Acrostic Sonnets

Umbrella: "Tipping Point, 94 Hamsters"

Valparaiso Poetry Review: "Tightrope Walker"

Victorian Violet Press: "Settling"

I am grateful to the editors who made these publications possible: Walter Ancarrow; Melissa Balmain; Kate Bernadette Benedict; Meredith Bergmann; Paul Bone and Rob Griffith; Edward Byrne; Pino Coluccio and Alexandra Oliver; Brad Davis and Heidi St. Jean; Wayne Dodd; Anna Evans, Jeff Holt, and Quincy Lehr; Kathryn Jacobs; Alex Pepple; Jennifer Reeser and Kalpna Singh-Chitnis; Willard Spiegelman; and David Yezzi.

"Juliet on Facebook" appeared in *Bully Pulpit,* White Violet Press, 2012. Many thanks to Karen Kelsay for the time and care on *Bully Pulpit* and to Paul Lake for the original publication in *First Things.*

I would also like to thank Kathryn Jacobs and Karen Kelsay for the opportunity to be a featured poet in *The Road Not Taken* and *Victorian Violet Press*, respectively.

I am grateful to Paul Bone and Rob Griffith for nominating "Jumping" for a Pushcart Prize and for featuring the poem on the *Measure* website. The poem was also printed as a limited edition broadside by Aralia Press, for which I thank Michael Peich.

"Nibbled to Death by Ducks" appeared in *The Best of Dial 2013;* "Misery Loves Company" and "Speaking Truth to Power" appeared in *The Best of Dial 2014.* My thanks to Pino Coluccio and Alexandra Oliver for this recognition and for the opportunity to appear with so many poets I admire.

A special issue of *The Rotary Dial* was devoted to my work: *The Bridgford Issue, America's First Lady of Form.* I wish to express my gratitude to Pino Coluccio and Alexandra Oliver once again. This issue came at a challenging and transformative time of my life, and there are not enough words to say how much this gesture meant to me then—and means to me now.

Contents

"But they are not together, the star twins, not really together."

"No, that is true, they are not tight up against each other in the sky, there is a tiny gap between them. That is the way of nature. Think of lovers. If lovers were tight up against each other all the time they would no longer need to love each other. They would be one. There would be nothing for them to want. That is why nature has gaps. If everything were packed tightly together, everything in the universe, then there would be no you or me or Ines. You and I would not be talking to each other right now, there would just be silence—oneness and silence. So, on the whole, it is good that there should be gaps between things, that you and I should be two instead of one."

The Childhood of Jesus, J. M. Coetzee

"Only connect."

E. M. Forster

I. Facebook

Unfriend

When *friend* became a verb, it was like Velcro—
A thing you *did* to someone else to stick.
To *un*friend is to pull apart, and then go.

You *friend*, and add them up: and have a friend glow.
You have a seven-hundred friend mystique.
When *friend* became a verb, it was like Velcro,

But sometimes you are bothered by the air flow.
An avatar alone can make you ache.
To *un*friend is to pull apart, and then go.

We'd like to *un* the world, but it's just not so,
Like e. e. cummings: *un*time and *un*forsake.
When *friend* became a verb, it was like Velcro.

A digital Descartes, I click, and then know:
And sometimes what I click is a mistake.
To *un*friend is to pull apart, and then go.

Within your Facebook page, you are the maestro,
But *"friend* and *un*friend*"* still means "give and take."
When *friend* became a verb, it was like Velcro.
To *un*friend is to pull apart, and then go.

Posting on the Wall, Facebook

I, one Snout by name, present a wall;
And such a wall, as I would have you think
That had in it a crannied hole or chink,
Through which the lovers Pyramus and Thisby
Did whisper often very seriously.

    Snout, *A Midsummer Night's Dream*

It's true the wall's more intimate, a Snout
Who represents the layering of stone,
And through which love will whisper its sweet route,
Away from public posts: cute sayings thrown

Into your scrolled-down life—the cult of ego—
The photos of the friends you think you know.
Write on your wall, sweet Pyramus and Thisbe.
Be anything you wanted love to be.

And others will peer in upon this tier,
The way we watched in Shakespeare's theatre.
It *is* more private than the public stream,
At night, mid-summer, and inside the dream.

Shhh. Type it. There. And once you post the moment,
The rest of us, who lurk and stalk, will comment.

Juliet on Facebook

I saw his Facebook picture, met for chat,
And then the two of us said *that was that:*
Except the world can always change online.
(I knew that already from his Rosaline.)

I felt the Capulets and Montagues
Were always asking the two of us to choose.
And all we wanted was the sweet IM
To jolt us in our bed at 3 AM.

Have you been bullied? That's what it was like:
The dread of all of the comments on the wall,
The feeling that they'll get you, one and all.
When he thought I was dead, it killed his soul.
I had to kill myself, and for his sake.
Now people can make comments: "Like. Dislike."

The Cyberspace Acrostic Sonnets:
Romeo and Juliet

Tybalt at Starbucks

Too much, too much, this Facebook feud. It friended,
Hated, fell in love: but Capulets
End any correspondence, however intended,
For Montagues, and Tybalt's temper sets
In motion the jabs and insults, little pricks
Espresso-fueled with chronic ADD.

Romeo is well aware of friend (and family) history,
Yearns for love, and also spiteful text:
Tybalt must pay the price for his Mercutio.

You think you know what cyberspace can do.

Bullies learn, of course, and posted lies
Alert the pack to fuel the victim's cries.
Learning those in doubt will not ask why,
Tybalt orders an espresso, then a chai.

Romeo and Juliet Fall in Love

Rosaline was once his love du jour.
Oh, Rosaline, I'll love you and forever.
More to the point, with Romeo in high school,
Exactitude in love is not a strict rule.
Oh, Juliet, I'll love you and forever.
Average all the hormones, phones, and coffee:
No wonder there's a shift. Now therapy
Delivers what was once done by the family.
Juliet loves his Facebook pictures, shares
Under the shifting Facebook scroll, and bears
Love, like an avatar and amulet.
I'm in love with you, Romeo. Luv u 4vr.
Enter her father, the grammarian set.
True love's not made by law, but by the letter.

Mercutio/Machismo

Mercutio defends his best friend in the storm.
Enter the Internet and all its rapiers.
Romeo, preoccupied with Juliet,
Considers his machismo. The high school set
Understands peer pressure keeps you warm,
Together with your girlfriend. Thus, the clique wars,
Internet-infused, and college bound.
Oh, Mercutio, how pettiness can spiral.
Initiating death comes from your games,
Sophisticated and yet with common names.
Death can unfriend, or it can go viral.
Everybody wants some drama, so pretend
All of this is in good fun. *Don't tell.*
Death, in the end, is always literal.

What the Parents Say

Parents make a lot of noise, but then
Admit they too were young and made mistakes.
Romeo, ignore the high-risk stakes.
Enter the paradox: you have sex when
Nobody believes you have it. Here's the rule:
Take the consequences, or take the pill.
Silence is the wheel that needs no grease.

And Juliet will stay innocent, fourteen;
Make dean's list, and then graduate from Brown.
No parties will ensue that bring police.
Everyone will act on what is true.
Shakespeare, of course, believed we rarely do.
Instead, we pass the code. Give us the lie,
And when you go to college, kiss good-bye.

The Nurse/Nana

Nobody thinks of Nana, but her girl,
And she will give J. everything: the pill,
New clothes, the latest iPhone, the way
Around her parents, and the cachet
In other parts of life. Nana does the laundry;
Navigates each bill, and every quandary.
The parents go to movies; drink their red,
Enjoy their middle age, and think they're dead.
Remember love, says Nana. Think of that
Forever when you think of her. Don't hate
Everything. You know it's not too late.
Remember her sweet smile, and combat
Every trace of cynicism while you surf
Sites that steal your souls, and all your worth.

Brother Lawrence

Not living in real time, in cyberspace,
Ordinary life does not relate to him.
To engineer false death to save romance
On any human level is absurd.
Father Lawrence, living in God's Time,
Together with the Ghost, and Son, and Word,
Has ancient texts informing his decision.

In the monastery, he makes jam,
Sings the chants and sways in ancient motion,
Waits for Lazarus-moments of "I-am."

Ordinarily, he's outside the passion
Rendered to his flock. He takes collection.
Lord help these children who will live the drama
Delivered by this plan: destined to bring trauma.

Alternative Universe

If they had never met, they would be bored,
Finding middle age, its wine, its Sunday brunch
Tantalizing at first. Then they would look
Homeward to their narratives, the hunch
Explicit in such looking back. Good Lord,
Youth looks good from here. Each classic book
Has not been read, all dreams unrealized,
And retirement packages haven't been apprised.
Drama's meant to underscore what's merely nice.
Nobody wants to say this is all there is.
That's the lie of later life, the biz
Married people don't share with the sweetly young
Endeavoring to know what's right and wrong.
To believe in love so much: that's worth the price.

II. The Love Song of the Middle-Aged Academic

Bad Writing

*Bad writing is always waiting. It comes to you—
you don't need to seek it out.*

William Logan

Like kamikaze pilots, or a drought—
A bully in your e-mail who's obsessed—
Bad writing waits for you and finds you out.

The adjectives and adverbs friend your site,
And once the CAPS show up, no Robert Frost.
Like kamikaze pilots, or a drought,

Such drama finds a path, and carves a route.
The kittens have a turn, the puppies next.
Bad writing waits for you and finds you out.

A mosquito waiting for the skin that's sweet,
It searches out your bedroom. Like a heist,
Like kamikaze pilots, or a drought,

With exclamations, it's immediate:
You're shouting on the page, and YOU ARE LOST!!!
Bad writing waits for you and finds you out.

You thought it was for truffles, but this snout
Burrows for your weakness, and your angst.
Like kamikaze pilots or a drought,
Bad writing waits for you and finds you out.

Dictionary

1.

It's big, it's bad, it's waiting to be used,
But there it sits, aloof from all that's happening.
(Perhaps in Scrabble there's an opening).

Once, fights broke out regarding who abused
The Webster's, AH, or the OED.
Now it's the invitation to the party.

2.

How quick is Google!   Who ever thought that pages
Would seem such work: the alphabet in stages,
And heavy in your hands, like lifting weights?
(It's like an old-school map in checking states.)

And yet to hold so much: this living text,
The reading without all special effects.

We stare across the room, like former lovers,
Who can't recapture life beneath the covers.

Gone Are the Libraries

Gone are the libraries, the card catalogues,
The homework that used to be eaten by dogs.
Gone are the libraries.

Gone are the magazines that very few read,
But poets all yearned for, to be garlanded.
Gone are the magazines.

Gone are the phone lines in dormitory halls,
Where love twists its signal and crying appalls.
Gone are the phone lines.

Gone are the letters, sent home from the war.
Calligraphied thank-yous, the airmail that tore.
Gone are the letters.

Gone are the typewriters that pecked at their truth,
But so is Joe DiMaggio, and so is Babe Ruth.
Gone are the typewriters.

Gone are the newspapers; gone are the shops
Where real food was sold by old moms and pops.
Gone are the newspapers.

Instead there is speed; and instead there is hype,
And, instead of live interviews, we set up our Skype.
Instead there is speed.

We find all this loss, when we're waiting or walking.
Nobody's thinking, and everyone's talking.
We find all this loss.

What have we done? Now we press and delete;
We sleep with our phones, and we text and we tweet.
What have we done?

Perfection Is the Enemy of the Good

A statement made by the chair of the English Department in
re-shaping the English Department curriculum, 2009-2010.

This shocks the public, wakes the grammar god,
As if espresso fired up each synapse.
Perfection is the enemy of the good.

Why else would teachers fill each page with red?
Why else would editors become obsessed?
This shocks the public, wakes the grammar god,

Who walks with Don Quixote and his steed,
And tilts at mediocrity, in relapse:
Perfection is the enemy of the good.

It's not the money, the long hours, or hybrid,
Bureaucracy and all its colored tapes
(This shocks the public, wakes the grammar god),

But a belief that excellence is fed.
And there it is: an *A*. Worth all these gripes.
Perfection is the enemy of the good:

It's like George Orwell in the neighborhood.
That's why we chose this discipline: for keeps.
This shocks the public, wakes the grammar god.
Perfection is the enemy of the good.

High School English Teachers

For Nicole Caruso Garcia

1.

Instead of focusing on summers off,
Let's focus on the nine months you have *on:*
By 7:00 you face Romeo and Juliet,
And every Montague and Capulet:
And that's the student body. Adolescence
Seethes with longing and idealism,
And, for protection, its own cynicism.

You bring the torch of love and common sense—
The books, dog-eared, you carry in your backpack;
You keep the stragglers from their straggling back.
A tender of each fire—with paper, kindling—
You gasp with them at each book's shocking ending.
You show the jeweldom of a well-wrought poem.
At 3:00 o'clock, they leave, and take you home.

2.

You will withstand the grammar jokes, the papers
Eaten by lost dogs; the phones, the Internet.
You're in the trenches with what you can get,
But you will ask them to look into vapors
Of their imaginations, shape their passions
Into the arc of history and traditions.

And when it happens, everyone looks up
At excellence with its silver loving cup:
A quavering sonnet, truth of someone's life,
The love of language shimmering like a knife,
The play whose drama whelms out from a peer.

In Frost-piles of your grading each semester,
You read for this: the subtle butterfly effects
In all their lives, whatever they do next.

3.

And when you're older, tired, and looking back
At all the morning hours, the Tupperware,
The weekends given to a point of grammar,
The parents awkward in the way of Prufrock,

The SAT and ACT, the grief
When first-choice colleges do not turn out;
The joy at *this* or *that* award, and *this* state bout,
The shimmer of the school year on each leaf,

There is a student who returns, and says,
"I am an English major because of you,"
A student who will see the *you* in you,
The one who fell in love with courtesies
Of language, tilted windmills, fought for youth.
You will say, "Thank you," and it is the truth.

The Love Song of the Middle-Aged Academic

And would it have been worth it, after all,
After the rubrics, the assessment, the ennui,
Among the Starbucks cups, among complacency,
Would it have been worth while,
To have bitten off the matter with a smile,
To have squeezed the universe into a ball
To roll it towards some overwhelming question,
To say: "I am an English major, come from the dead,
Come back to tell you all, I shall tell you all"—
If an associate dean, with another e-mail before bed,
        Should say: "That is not what I meant at all;
        That is not it, at all."

And would it have been worth it, after all,
Would it have been worth while,
After the department meetings, and the cutbacks, and the weekend
   retreats,
After the outcomes, the goals not to be confused with outcomes,
   each petty war—
All this, and so much more?—
It is impossible to say just what I mean!
But as if my Healthy U threw the nerves in patterns on a screen:
Would it have been worth while
If one, at another Friday meeting, then should drawl,
And turning toward the window, should say:
        "That is not it at all,
        That is not what I meant, at all."

No! I am not Emily Dickinson, nor was meant to be;
Am a VIDA poet, an editor that will do
To swell the progress, announce a Facebook post or two,
Away from print (online an easier tool),
From a retro age, glad to be of use,
Risk taking but meticulous;

Full of high sentence, but a bit obtuse;
At times, indeed, almost ridiculous—
To still believe in school.

I grow old . . . I grow old . . .
I shall wear black pants until my last poem's sold.

Shall I wear hair short or long? Do I dare to eat a peach?
I shall wear a Talbots dress, and walk upon the beach.
I have heard the old books singing, each to each.

I do not think that they will sing to me.

I have seen Virginia Woolf upon the waves
Combing the white hair of the waves blown back
When the wind blows the water white and black.

We have lingered in the chambers of the sea
With heroes wreathed with seaweed red and brown
Till administrators wake us, and we drown.

III. Human Interest Stories

Tipping Point, 94 Hamsters

Massachusetts man gives up 94 hamsters

Lawrence, Mass: A Massachusetts man has turned over 94 hamsters to a local animal shelter, telling officers he was running out of room in his apartment. A Lawrence animal control officer said the man was overwhelmed.

Associated Press

You won't all fit inside this tidy space,
And so you'll need to seek out other homes.
You cram the edges, the corridors of place,
And line the cliff-top edges of our dreams.

And was it just that he had had "enough,"
The way that Howard Hughes one day said no
To ice cream flavors he was tired of,
Or was it something primitive, the slow

Dawning that the hamsters, hundredfold,
Might be like Tribbles on the Enterprise,
Or adolescent hormones in disguise?
Was ninety-four the perfect hamster yield

To make him look up from his human lack,
A hundred eighty-eight eyes looking back?

Oh, Rats

China's solution to plague of 2 billion rats:
truck them to restaurants.

    The Daily Mail

Most people would be heebie-jeebied by
Two billion rats that sneak up in a body:
Eight billion feet that run on hunger, greed.

The solution is to ask, "Which one will feed?"

This question turns the mass, for hungry people,
To meat that offers protein, adds to fat
(And makes a person much more like his cat).

If people don't know what to do, it's simple.

Eat, and eat again. It's all procedure
Like the worst bureaucracy. The rules are there
To numb, to make what is essential *non-*.
Bon appétit. Chew up what is available.
Don't worry about edges that you nibble.
You know it's easy. Grab your fork. Come on.

No

Deadly snakes hatch in toddler's closet

This is the snake effect, not butterfly:
When parenting and sense have gone awry,
Some lethal brown snakes fierce and warm with hatching,
And no one, over toddling age, is watching.

Of course, you can step back. Who hasn't done
A thing that seems as innocent, a collection
Of shells, or fireflies, or dandelions?
Who leans toward danger: not just mighty pythons,

But rabid dogs, or rats, or baby gators?
It seems all right until investigators
Ask how deadly snakes were hatched with clothes,
The diapers, velcroed shoes, and goodness knows

What else inside the darkness of the closet.
It makes a person pause, and then to posit.

Chew on This

The horrible anger you feel at hearing someone
chewing is called misophonia

"Must you chew gum?" is what Norma Desmond said.
I thought that this was part of paranoia.
Instead it was untreated misophonia,
Like someone slurping up a chocolate malted.

You long for quiet, in your heightened state,
And realize you want to kill your mate.
What's soft to eat? you think. No cereal.
No nuts. No food in earth time. Nothing real.

Candy canes are out, if they'll be chewed.

It's not just that the behavior's rude:
You don't like being so aware of teeth,
The lives of humans going on beneath.

The clue to understanding this idea?
Remove the "onomat-" from every "-poeia."

Ghosting

*After reading an article that Charlize Theron has ended her
relationship with Sean Penn by "ghosting"*

Ghosting: *the act of never returning calls, text messages,
or emails*

Now this is what we do. No tears, good-bye.
We simply find a convenient alibi.
No long nights crying on a jagged pillow.
We Casper and we Ghost; we find a hollow
Through which we slip ourselves, in our new art.

For this is how our love will come apart.

It is so easy to erase a name:
There. What-if is now *what was.* No blame.
It's nothing to pin aspiration on.
(No need to think about a thing that's gone.)

We forget, like Casper, that there's no suicide
For friendly ghosts. There is no sin or pride.
The more we look, the more we shall not find.
What once was love was never cruel, nor kind.

IV. Famous News Stories

Lindbergh Baby Kidnapping*

1. The Baby

It's dark here in the leaves, and I am cold.
I wonder what will happen to me now.
I want to be back home, not in this field.
My father is like stone, and he will punish.

The sounds I hear approach, and then they vanish.

This is like a fairy tale: for gold
A child is given. Then there's the rescue.
I'm tired of being put outside, compelled.

What is that coming toward me? I think wings,
Or life undone into a thousand things.
The pain is like an airplane, its propeller.
I wonder if it's part of my own failure.
I'd like to go back home. I am so tired.
I'm left beneath the stars and undesired.

*After a nation-wide search, the baby was eventually found, having been clubbed to
death within five miles of his house.

2. Anne, Some Years Later

I'm left beneath the stars and undesired.
I'd like to go back home: I am so tired.
I wonder if it's part of my own failure.
The pain is like an airplane, its propeller,
Or life undone into a thousand things.

What is that coming toward me? I think wings.

I'm tired of being put outside, compelled.
A child is given. Then there's the rescue.
This is like a fairy tale: for gold—

The sounds I hear approach, and then they vanish.

My heart is like a stone, and it will punish.

I want to be back home, not in this field.
I wonder what will happen to me now.
It's dark here in the leaves, and I am cold.

Patty Hearst Sonnet

Tell everybody that I'm smiling, that I feel free and strong
and I send my greetings and love to all the sisters and brothers
out there (on being arrested for bank robbery).

    Patty Hearst

I remember watching you on video:
You robbed the bank, the focus of the scene.
What did you feel? I didn't seem to know.
I was transfixed by your strange glamour, though.

I remember you were grainy, but still you:
As if they made you up, but brought you down.
There was something exciting, in what you'd been through
(The crease of media ambivalence
Would voyeurize me with experience).
I didn't know what you were going to do.

In that one moment, to mythologize,
You became another person for our eyes.
An heiress/outlaw, carrying your gun,
Released from our constraints, you now had none.

In the News: Bill Cosby

A word to the wise ain't necessary—it's the stupid ones that need advice.

Bill Cosby

Anagram:

A word to the ladies, evident by nasty tactics he uses, is: Don't be alone with this creep.

Kevin Dopart, Style Invitational, *The Washington Post*

It is all about what's rearranged: the timing,
The age, the famous versus the acolyte.
To hear the stories, and the public shaming,
Pulls up the rock, and shines a public light.

Some people are exactly what they say;
Some take the mantle of celebrity,
And with a silky lining, and soft voice,
Create illusions, and remove all choice.

Compartments make it possible for the jaded.

One morning, to awake, and wonder what will save.
The drugged-up coffee is a narrative
With epic feelings, doors pulled shut. They waited.

The Handmaid's Tale, by Atwood, speaks aloud:
A single woman's voiceless, not a crowd.

Telling It

1.

The way she's telling it, it seems not true,
The way that horror can so often do:
The way that she was tired, the way she cried,
The way he kindly offered her a ride.

The way ten years passed, the way she learned
A swinging light bulb meant that he returned,
The way her soul was chained, and starved, and beaten
(One moment she was lost and then forgotten).

The way that she emerged in blinking light,
And there was the world, not wrong or right,
But waiting, like all time, for what was next.
She would reveal the bareness of her facts:
The children lost, the years—and in plain sight.
The way she lived like this, just down the street.

2.

The way she lived like this, just down the street:
The children lost, the years—and in plain sight.
She would reveal the bareness of her facts.
But waiting, like all time, for what was next,
There was the world, not wrong or right,
The way that she emerged in blinking light.

One moment she was lost and then forgotten,
The way her soul was chained, and starved, and beaten.
A swinging light bulb meant that he returned:
The way ten years passed, the way she learned

The way he kindly offered her a ride,
The way that she was tired, the way she cried.
The way that horror can so often do,
The way she's telling it, it seems not true.

Tighttrope Walker

For Philippe Petit

Your foot along the outline of all space,
You know the God that others never face,
The precipice of all morality,
The lion's breath of your mortality.

You turn. They are so small down there. So round
Their gapes and moans: as if they understood
Just now the math of what your spangled heart
Could do. It's physical, this circus art,

The *this* times *that,* the braided coil you walk
A little closer to the clouds. Reverse
Icarus, you take the tremble of your curse
And feel it with your toe. *Ooh! Magnifique!*

Meanwhile the dotted line of air you try
Holds: see-through carpet, narrow with the sky.

Jumping

ten years later

Sometimes I think of them, when I am kept
Awake at night. It was a workday morning
When they died, an ordinary morning when they leapt.
They made it look so easy, therefore earning
Our respect, like a complicated skill.
You can forget it was not easy at all.

They didn't seem to pause. Like cherubim—
The office staff, accountants, businessmen—
Within the ash of morning, they would glisten,

Remembering that love's a crucible,
And wishing—as did we—for a hand (something!)
To tap the heavens, see if God's at home.

And fell. Such quiet in their terror-song.
We could not look away, watched far too long.

V. Clichés

Nibbled to Death by Ducks

They won't leave you alone, but you think this
Is all they'll do to you: a soft distraction
Draining your life. Suction, not satisfaction.
Just one more thing. They are your only business.

Meanwhile the things that matter are now lost,
Your life surrendered to what matters least.
On a far, wide field stands your once-success;

Once, you swam in thoughts of happiness.

You're older now, and also cynical.
It's easy to make fun of those who care.
Your wishes hang on falling stars, your jar
Of insects dead upon the windowsill.

The ducks settle in: they're soft and sweet.
They wear the look of those with plenty to eat.

Falling Through the Cracks

Think cockroach, think the serendipitous
Slither of the things that you don't see
Or want to see. There's an apocalypse
Happening at night. You get up and make your coffee.

Later, when your car stumbles—pothole?
Earthquake?—you think you could fall through.
What lives down there, waiting in the sinkhole?
Breathless, you pause: and then you follow through,

But underneath you feel the rancid movement
Of all decay. Bananas gain their spots.
Relationships have reached the turning moment,
Unburied hatchets ready. The dry earth begets
Emptiness—flexing one muscle, then another,
The zigzags breaking the back of your mother.

Misery Loves Company

Misery is having a party tonight.
Bent-Out-of-Shape is there, and so is Malice.
Everybody's looking for a fight.

Whose marriage has fallen? Whose field has blight?
Gossip prances in between Bitter and Jealous.
Misery is having a party tonight.

The hors d'oeuvres are laced with bile and plight,
And the wine that is served is Napa Salacious.
Everybody's looking for a fight.

Misery is married to Just-Served-You-Right;
The children are bitchy, each argument specious.
Misery is having a party tonight.

Come in, and sit down. You're a welcome sight.
Lust swings through the door, and hits on Curvaceous.
And everybody's looking for a fight.

In walk Small-Minded, Cold-Blooded, and Hate.
Martinis are handed to Sterling and Cautious.
Misery is having a party tonight,
And everybody's looking for a fight.

Well, Pinch My Toes and Call Me a Jelly Doughnut

Actually, don't. I would prefer another kind
Of moniker: Kefir, a Crepe, Croissant
(Some other type for the specialty gourmand),
Espresso. Don't reach out for pinch or paint,

As far as toes go. It's an awe-struck no-show.
What kind of news brings out this odd remark,
Like kissing cousins put on Noah's Ark,
Eccentric closeness marking what they know?

Collectibles of human hair! The words
To television songs from 1950!
Someone's had a baby; flung the shards
Of a marriage in the old burn barrel.
Touch my arm; look in my eyes. Try lofty.
Try handshakes. Cardamom, then Caramel.

All That Glitters Is Not Gold

When you realize that you just don't matter;
When you see that good and evil link their hands.
When you see that all your youthful dreams will shatter,
That no one really understands;

When you wonder where *you've* been, your voice naïve;
When you think about where all your years have gone;
When you find that it is easier to believe
Than risk the thought of nothingness, alone;

When you see how people face this: drink and laughter;
Cruelty; all the drama pettiness can know;
The brief affairs, the taunting ever-after,
The jealousy that breeds from bad luck, and from sorrow;

You want to start all over; pry the thing apart;
Remove the narcissism of your hot *I-am.*
Find the line that takes the last from its first start,
And be the lamb.

All Hell Has Broken Loose

And fallen off the hinge. Hell is about looking,
And they are looking back: the kidnapped girls
Living at the end of time, chewing on their nails
And despair.

One day they start to run.

His eyes

Are flat, and this is what you're looking at.
Hell is, you see, the place instead of empathy.

A hollow form, it's pain that makes him warm.

In the interrogation room, this man is breaking.

Babies dying in a hot car, the dice in hot palms:
Hell is a place of crimes instead of qualms.

Rational and cold, a paper shredder,
Hell is where things are torn apart for better
Or worse. Hell is, above all, mechanical.
They twist the screws each time to make him tell.

Speaking Out of Both Sides of Your Mouth

This is tongue twisting, with an evil edge:
The cartoon devil saying the opposite
Of what *you've* said, you with your Boy Scout badge.

This is how certain leaders prosper, get
A foothold: friendly, genial, dare we
Say liars? No. We say *not-truth, not-right,*

The way we used to lie awake, nightlight
In its little place, pretending infancy.
Each side of your mouth says something about

The world: One is the pretty way, like a lamb
Sparkling its wobbly haunch. The other route
Is realpolitik, with Uncle Sam

Pointing at you, and then pointing at us.
We call this moment trust and lack of trust.

Benign Neglect

The King looks out upon his enterprise.
He's mild and good, and saddened by the lies
Of those who try to take his kingdom. He tries
To rule by inspiration, and through ease.

Yet envy drives the force of others who
Take every opportunity to do
A wrong to him. The lawyers try to sue;
And those with malice undermine what's true.

Meanwhile, the King, whose vision sides with grandeur,
Presents the world, much like a teacher does.
The people love him, while the huntsmen swarm.
Which is better: life dreamt or as it is?
They want to see him fail, this kindly leader.
How else see fear as comfort and the norm?

Speaking Truth to Power

First, they thanked her for her honesty.
They liked that she was passionate, sincere.
She found old files. She reported, as her duty.
Yet little things began to bother her.

Their wings were bland and gray: and like a shadow,
There they were, officious, writing down
Her violation of Rule 1b. Ditto
D, and f, and constantly rewritten.

She thought that it must be her imagination.
She tried to work.

                    Then, they began to scare her.

They showed up at her meetings and her office.
They smiled, and told her to do much more with less.
They moved her to a remote, secure location
All by herself. And then they took her chair.

VI. Ghosts

Ghosts

There are so many wound stories. . . . What we notice in the stories is the nearness of the wound to the gift. . . . There is always the return. And the wound will take you there.

Jeanette Winterson

Of course you can go back.
Your fourth grade teacher, her hair
Like cotton candy spun over a fitted suit,
Is weeping. Her husband was killed in a plane crash.
All that year, your class wandered
In the shock of her grief—waited minutes for answers,
Covered hands with paste and then peeled it
With undivided attention, learned this flat
And scorched-out desert was a place to live.
Meanwhile, the other fourth grade teacher twirled you
Because, during the game of 7Up, he saw you looking.
Afterwards, you wanted to burn that dress,
The bottom half red, the top half a newsprint pattern
Because you loved words so much it was almost shame.
Ghosts link arms in ways you never expected,
Like paper dolls from different eras, mismatched
In pinafores, miniskirts, and homemade scrawls.
Today, your grade school is a meat packing plant,
With a cow sculpture lit by a spotlight on the lawn.
Then, you had so many Girl Scout badges it was like
You were on fire, but you were just a cat in a bag,
Clawing to get out. You would be in your back yard
Rubbing two sticks together, then diagramming
The genealogies in the Bible, then sewing a straight seam.
When the neighbor didn't pick you up from school,
And you tried to hitchhike home, you remember
The way your mother's hands shook. You didn't know
Children were picked up and not returned,
Found years later in abandoned freezers or tossed out

Like chewed-on supper bones. Riding the junior high school bus,
Someone asked, "Why is your mother up in that apple tree?,"
And there she was, in her robe, making sure you had made it.
And the trees are gone, and the teachers you looked up to,
Their ideas like a Grail. In such a world,
There were extremes. Even if it was one hundred
Percent correct, if you spelled a word wrong, it was an *F*.
The Job of spelling, you had to make a decision,
So you learned to spell with an entomologist's delicacy.
At school, some of the books were so old
Their very portrayal sold you the classics.
You thought people on the East Coast read books
In rows of breathless infinity, surrounded by stone lions
With impassive expressions and regal and stupendous paws.
Now here's your mother chasing a horse
Down the highway. What did your family need with a horse?
And she would save it because that's what people did.
Later, after her stroke, she said that moments
Never come back, but she wasn't talking about that one;
She meant dreams: roseate, like your eyes half closed.
One night, you watched Billy Graham on TV
By yourself, on your knees. In your play about Simon Bolivar,
In your powder blue pantsuit, you knew you could go back.
The room was quiet, the cardboard taste of milk
On everyone's lips. You didn't know *whose* wound it was,
But you crawled into the time machine anyway.
At the end, you took the hands of all the ghosts dancing.

See

It's not what people *don't* see; it's what they see
And live with, the lion without courage
Biting on his own fist. And when the truth is presented—
Clear, shabby, with innocence blinking on its own tears—
No one wants to hear about the gods
That are not gods, the statues covered with gilt
Instead of gold.

People who are hurt grow up to hurt others—
We know this—so why are we surprised
About the boy pushed against the bare wood
Of a changing room, and how his cry changes nothing
About the world, but his own,
How underneath a sheen of goodness
There are the things that, daily, happen to people?
Even the priests say, as one said to me,
That "everybody has a side."

You see what I mean?
We all know the stories:
The fat kid who grows up to hurt successful women,
Bullying them over the Internet;
The boy in the changing room who pulls his swimming trunks
Up over his shaking hips, and years later in a college dorm room
Writes to his teacher—the same woman bullied by the grown-up
    fat boy,
The teacher who turns out to be me—
That one day he was broken.
He still knows the exact smell of the changing room
And the feeling of that wood against his face.
He had trouble walking afterwards,
And what could he say? And if he did,

What would happen? That's what they knew
In Eden, when the skin of the apple broke,
And they walked out the gate.

So it was for the boy.
The world went on: the smell of hot dogs,
The spurt of mustard—and how the older boy
Treated him to both. He threw up afterwards.
Don't you see? What can his teacher do, weeping at her narrow
    desk,
Picturing his blank eyes, the way he cannot focus,
The way sorrow puts its feet under the door?
He wants to be the boy he was
Before everything and nothing changed.
It is the nothing that has killed him, and she cannot give
Him the gift he wants. She can correct his grammar;
She can applaud the honesty that pounds in her chest.
She knows this even while she waits for another message from the
    bully
Who is the chair of her department, who will cc others
So they can witness, and take pleasure in,
His delicate and dagger-like assault.
Later, he becomes a dean for his "proactive leadership."

See? We say we want the truth,
But when the statues fall,
And they have lost all the old meanings—
Relics of our worship, tenders of desire—
We don't like the absence left behind.
We side with cruelty because we know it—
The way we know the inside of our own mouths,
And tongue their intimate structures—
Because of all the things we teach each other
We learn that best.

God Is Not the Status Quo

religion on the superficial level. . . . God is the status quo.

Thomas Merton [arguing against God as the "status quo"]

You watch the petty fires of bully bosses;
The rumors people stoke with gas and matches.
There always is a scapegoat, always masses
To do the dirty work that evil hatches.

And God's the opposite: not administrations,
Not politics, but single ministrations.
If courage were not hard, more people would—
Instead of going along—do what they should.

God takes the body, and God takes the ego.
It's not that "everybody has a side,"
But that Christ took a certain way, and died.
You can eat him, dream him, pray him, know him,
Half human being, and half cherubim.
His definition shatters status quo.

Spite

How people sit and nurse their private hates,
The way that heiresses accrue estates,
Their mop-head dogs bejeweled with pedigrees,
And Versace dresses high above their knees.

And usually this feral lick of spite
Is traced to one small thing—innocuous—
But has inside a moral precipice.
The fall is thrilling. Wingless, cool, and right:

But hot inside the heart. So intricate:
Like Darwin stumbling on a nameless creature—
Millennia inside its architecture—
Adapting to a need. You grow to meet it,

And forget. The muscle in your shoulder's tight.
The gap you feel there once was filled with light.

Hero

1.

Sometimes there's a clamor for the glamour of the hero.
It does not matter whether it's false or true.
We want to eat you raw, then feel the awe.
We want to trade this feeling for our sorrow.

We have done everything for the first time.
Like all the others, we have Eden, loss.
Betrayal's squeeze has felt the same to us.
That's why we need you, your unvarnished name.

Forgiveness is a gilded tablecloth:
You taught us that it's *how* you think, not *why*.
Invariably, all life has passed us by.
We open wide. We hold you in our teeth:
Holy, dusty, less like the ground than air.
You are the proof that life is never fair.

2.

You are the proof that life is never fair.
Wholly dusty, less like the ground than air,
We open wide; we hold you in our teeth.
Invariably, all life has passed us by.

You taught us that it's *how* you think, not why
Forgiveness is a gilded tablecloth.

That's why we need *you*, your unvarnished name.
Betrayal's squeeze has felt the same to us.
Like all the others, we have Eden, loss.

We have done everything for the first time.

We want to trade this feeling for our sorrow.
We want to eat you raw, then feel the awe.
It does not matter whether it's false or true.

Sometimes there's a clamor for the glamour of the hero.

Ventriloquist

Which one of us is wood? Which hand? Which finger
Controls the bargain, cops the feel, to linger
Along the other's trunk, the living tree?
Which one of us is you, and which is me?

Which lifts the lift, and worms the moral worm?
Which makes the audience, sunshiny, to squirm
At what unsettles them in hypnotism?
The bat of free will's eye, and its great schism.

At night, I keep you in your coffin box,
The way Donne practiced in his funeral shroud.
You speak life's moral emptiness aloud.
You slap your knees; your dance unlocks
My cat's cradle, spider-baby, incubus.
Such sticky love designs and sutures us.

Settling

It's hard to know the moment that you settle.
Yet one day you see things are just not right.
And then do you go on, or pick your battle?

It's like a snake before you hear its rattle;
It's like the light before it doesn't light.
It's hard to know the moment that you settle:

At first, it's just that you might hurt a little,
Or that you find you're shifting in your seat.
And then do you go on, or pick your battle?

You're worried that the *fine*'s gone from your fettle,
And who would want you now? You should just wait.
It's hard to know the moment that you settle.

The drops heat up and shimmer in the kettle.
The whistle blows. To pour or hesitate?
And then do you go on, or pick your battle?

To stay or go will prove your moral mettle.
The question is which one will be your fate.
It's hard to know the moment that you settle,
And then do you go on, or pick your battle?

Done

1.

Darling, you scared me. You said you were done.
It was like breathing tears or tasting rain.
Trembling, you wanted to start all over again.
This is how history's written and rewritten.

There are things you learn that you can never say,
But people say them. They say them every day.
They say things as if they just discovered pain:
"I've never felt like this," "She knows how to listen."

Darling, you scared me. This is another you.
A you that's grown out of the *used-to-you:*
The *fresh-start you.* This is the *take-a-breather you.*
It's hard to sit here, so erased from you.

This is the reason that most people lie.
Whatever has grown cold will only die.

2.

Whatever has grown cold will only die.
This is the reason that most people lie.

It's hard to sit here, so erased from you,
The *fresh-start you.* This is the *take-breather you,*
A you that's grown out of the *used-to-you.*
Darling, you scared me. This is another you:
"I've never felt like this," "She knows how to listen."

They say things. As if they just discovered them.
But people say them: they say them every day.
There are things you learn that you can never say.

This is how history's written and rewritten.
Trembling, you wanted to start all over again.
It was like breathing tears or tasting rain,
Darling. You scared me. You said you were done.

The Fence

One day, it seems they all look old.
One day, it seems it didn't matter.
One day, it seems what once was gold
Was really not. The something better

You always thought was coming next
Was like the rumored farthest hill.
Why was it just the same again?
Why was the optimism shrill?

Why did you then look up and see
How people came and people went,
And no one cared? But meanwhile money
Bought the system, and what it meant.

You lived your life in innocence,
And had a pretty child. You wept.
They depend on folks like you. The fence?
It grew around you while you slept.

The Past

The past is what you're looking at:
Sepia, historical, and lost.
Emotions mold and shatter it.

You built this house and shuttered it,
And yet, inside, there was a cost.
The past is what you're looking at.

You thought it didn't matter that
There was a time you weren't your best.
Emotions mold and shatter it.

Are you defending how you acted?
That you weren't different from the rest?
The past is what you're looking at

(The worst, you hope, has been redacted).
While, still, you hope your life is blessed,
Emotions mold and shatter it.

The charm of cruelty is to bear it:
But you've sold out like Dr. Faust.
The past is what you're looking at,
Emotions' mold. Now shatter it.

About the Author

Kim Bridgford is the director of Poetry by the Sea: A Global Conference. As editor of *Mezzo Cammin,* she was the founder of The *Mezzo Cammin* Women Poets Timeline Project, which was launched at the National Museum of Women in the Arts, and has held events at the Pennsylvania Academy of the Fine Arts and at Fordham-Lincoln Center. The author of eight books of poetry, including *Epiphanies* and *Doll,* she is the recipient of fellowships from the Connecticut Commission on the Arts, the National Endowment for the Arts, and the Ucross Foundation. Her collaborative three-volume work with visual artist Jo Yarrington on Iceland, Venezuela, and Bhutan, *The Falling Edge,* is forthcoming. Bridgford has appeared in *The New York Times, The Washington Post, The Philadelphia Inquirer, The Connecticut Post,* on NPR, and in various headline news outlets. She wrote the introduction to Russell Goings' *The Children of Children Keep Coming: An Epic Griot Song,* and joined Goings in ringing the closing bell of the New York Stock Exchange, the week before the first Obama inauguration. Bridgford has been called "America's First Lady of Form."